The Book of Mirrors

# The Book of Mirrors

## Yun Wang

THE WHITE PINE PRESS POETRY PRIZE, #26

WHITE PINE PRESS / BUFFALO, NEW YORK

White Pine Press
P.O. Box 236
Buffalo, NY 14201
www.whitepine.org

Publication of this book was supported with public funds from a grant from the New York State Council on the Arts, with the support of Governor Andrew M. Cuomo and the New York State Legislature, a State Agency, and with funds from the Amazon Literary Partnership.

Printed and bound in the United States of America.

Book design: Elaine LaMattina

ISBN 978-1-945680-47-2

Library of Congress Control Number: 2020952145

# Acknowledgments

Grateful acknowledgments go to the following journals and anthologies in which these poems (sometimes in earlier versions) first appeared:

*Abstract Magazine TV:* "Forecasts," "Sam's Plan."
*Blue Fifth Review:* "Black Roses."
*Cimarron Review:* "The Beetle from Outer Space," "Neighbors in Bathrobes," "Transformation."
*Earth Tones: Creative Perspectives on Ecological Issues:* "Migration."
*Even the Daybreak: 35 Years of Salmon Poetry:* "Seascape at South Padre Island."
*Poetry Midwest:* "Shadow Test."
*Prairie Schooner:* "Immortality," "The Visitation," "Casanova: A Translation from Fellini."
*Salamander Magazine:* "Face on Mars," "August Dream," "The Mirror's Edge."
*Valparaiso Poetry Review:* "Winter Seascape."
*Voices International:* "San Francisco Bay at Night."
*Waves on One Sea: Contemporary Poems from Ireland and the U.S.* (Salmon Poetry Press): "Nocturne II," "Minuet."

The following poems (some of them in earlier versions) first appeared in the chapbook *Horse by the Mountain Stream* (Word Palace Press, 2016):
"Horse by the Mountain Stream," "Superstition of a Caged Bird," "Sirius," "Cleopatra's Dream," "Snow Angel," "Gifted with Beauty," "Sam's Questions," "An Ancient Ice Bridge Breaks," "Contact," "Epiphany."

The author grateful acknowledges helpful comments on early versions of some of the poems from J.L. Jacobs, Paul Portuges, Marc Herant, and especially Carol Koss and Valerie Duff, who also provided constructive feedback on an earlier version of the book manuscript. The author's son, Samuel Ming Wang-Koenigsberg, contributed unflinching critique on a number of the poems in earlier versions.

*For my son Sam*
my best friend
and harshest critic

# Table of Contents

## I

## II

# III

# IV

*The Book of Mirrors*

I

# Face on Mars

The path was there before anyone
human trod it

A random formation in nature

On the lofty cross the white-gowned angel
lifted her heels

At your finger's touch
the wreath of daisies
turns to ashes
shadow of a candlestick

Your eyes wake from darkness

You were told it was all in you
deep at the bottom
nothing but revelation

How many times have you died
and lived to see
the angel shedding whiteness
the tomb of millennia open

# Superstition of a Caged Bird

Invisible fibers bind all of us here
Phantoms walk upon the trees
Green eyes of men follow me
A school of luminescent fish

Sunset reveals a scarlet net

I hear the gossip of flowers
insatiable in their lust
Consider the cages that are our bodies

When the touch came in such tenderness
I was stirred into maddening fear
If I were free
where would I go
There is only the infinity of darkness
strewn with eyes of the dead

A path is born at sunrise

Eyes of the living follow me
between dreams of oblivion
Phantoms come in a whistle

I am drawn to the shore
watch ponies dance in the waves
A little girl laughs in the wild
green of the water
The cage strains

The air is haunted by crushed petals

# Cleopatra's Dream

The sphinxes whisper each to each
A white cat creeps
through the black mirror

The Nile sends a breeze in flirtation
to sleek maidens half-wrapped in silk
Fair Antony frets
not knowing
his own destiny

An emerald flower withers
on bleeding sand

## Regret

If I were a tree
I would never have shed
all my leaves
for the caress of sunset

and stepped naked
into that moonless
starless night

A trap embraced me
I had no voice

# Sapphire

She can't take her eyes off the sapphire framed by the highrise window. A flock of geese honk past. She is seized by the desire to leap after them. The cat combs her long ebony hair with its tongue.

"Do not go into the light," Grandmother whispered behind a white lace veil, in the abandoned garden at the end of a long dry riverbed. She had never met her grandmothers, except for the one from a fairy tale.

"Do not wake while flying," she sings to herself. Traffic rankles a forest of towering mirrors.

The cat is uprooting her hair, trying to free itself. White swans in flight dissolve into a dark sea punctured by stars. She stomps her foot on the brake. The scarlet car dashes through drowned streets.

Lightning slashes open the sapphire. She jumps out of bed. The phone is ringing louder than a fire alarm. "Please check all your faucets and sinks," says the night watchman. "The apartment beneath you is flooded."

## Bach's Chaconne

Streams meander beneath a gibbous moon
Teardrop doors open from shadows

Pearl garlands shimmer on the sea

Naked tree limbs burst into green buds
Mountains sigh in efflorescence

# Black Roses

The Universe echoes in the marble ballroom
Each time a new tide of static

Fizzes from specks in a map of the sky
Each speck the shrunken image of a galaxy

Great walls of galaxies swell in the static
Each galaxy the luminous stamen of a dark flower

&ast;  &ast;  &ast;

Cold flames of fragrance
singe my senses
My life evaporates
as I gaze into these roses

&ast;  &ast;  &ast;

The man I admire died decades ago
can't unmake what he made
He invented labels for poets
without their knowledge

Muses flowered and withered
Some bit his hand and left
Others wept at his grave

There must be God somewhere
maneuvering all that mess into stars
The caseworker leans back in his chair
fingers laced

&ast;      &ast;      &ast;

"When you go for interviews
you have to be tough      Lie
if need be      Assure them you are
a very dedicated cosmologist
Even if a child happens
it would not affect your research"

&ast;      &ast;      &ast;

Beneath the stars      many astrologers
Two of them accosted me
The man smirked and held my waist
Told me there would have been signs
if I were gifted in poetry
The woman read my mind with a stack
of cards trimmed in Egyptian blue

&ast;      &ast;      &ast;

"I dislike the violence in this poem
It's not like you      the rape and the plunge
of dagger into someone's throat
But I like this stanza
I love the vultures
When I die I want to be fed to the vultures"

&ast;      &ast;      &ast;

"It's the flower which victimizes
the insect" shouts the blonde nurse
She insists that Hans Christian Andersen
hated children and wrote "The Happy Prince"
to scare the little monsters

Somewhere church bells peal
interrupting a ring of ardent poets
Down the street an old woman pulls up her car
Three towers topped by glowing crosses
behind the raven black street

# Nocturne I

The one I have waited for
will not be coming

Only dogs and thieves

The moon bleeds
in the hilltop pond

Bamboos strangle my hut
A lamp burns for no one

Should I burn down the bridge

# Muse with a Brown Paper Bag

Wear a boa of black tulips and nothing else
Examine dirt through an electron-tunneling microscope
Knock on a lichen door of limestone boulders in a jade river
Hunt fossil ferns and shoulder the bones of flying dinosaurs

Who is afraid of poetry

Rap to the beat of bat wings in a cave
Lecture rapists about the spirituality of sex
Commune with the dead by living their darkest fantasies
Consider cutting off one of your ears

The doorknob is a cat's voice

Poetry is a spread of black and white photos
of loners in leather and lace
Muse is a grumpy old man with wooden doorknobs
He replaces your doorknob with his own

The doorknob tortures you

You dig up the floor get splinters in search of purple diamonds
You shape blood-mixed dirt into a bead necklace
hang it around your neck and pose in a cemetery
The doorknob bursts into laughter

# Liebestraum

A tree blooms in the night sky
Each star a flower forbidden

A stranger plays the piano
pulses light to shadow

A million trees bend with weight
of gravitating dark matter

Each star's love unrequited
Every planet a path not taken

The stranger's coat darkens the night
Strands of hair brush his pale face

Winter plum blossoms stir starlight
A scented portal in time

In the singing of forgotten dreams
I step through and drown

## Poppies

The heart waits to be lit from within
To laugh with translucent petals

\*          \*          \*

The sun overspills golden cups
nodding into the wind

\*          \*          \*

The heart waits for rain to grow
a field of soft flames

\*          \*          \*

Mark fleshy blades' song before sunset
shrinks the million golden goblets

## Sirius

A school of sardines drills into
a curving wall of hanging water

Beach sunflowers whisper
retreating sun
Seedpods adorn my feet
with thorns

Blue sea rolls dark green waves
into billions of white horses

the cavalry of oblivion

A starfish becomes a sand dollar
Mountains turn to sand

I search the deserted beach
for an invisible sign
as the Milky Way turns

II

# The Nun and the Prince

Winter plum blossoms blazed
The birds of luminous moments
perched in vermilion plumage

Around them the snow
white as her intention
She played chess
with the dashing prince

A gust of wind rained down
flame-red petals on snow

The surge of incense smoke
urged her to return
to meditation

He smiled as he bid her farewell
cradling a branch of scarlet blossoms

That smile stirred her for years
melted the snow in her dream

One night she woke from the dream
in the arms of a robber
who had broken into the nunnery

# Nine Springs

A dark stranger came to the ancient capital, swept the city off its feet with the reputation of his Yang staff. It would not soften or break, even when tied to a running carriage. Courtesans rushed to entertain him.

The queen regent summoned the stranger to her bedchamber, tested him. She instructed that he be received into the palace, registered as a eunuch.

The little prince resented the moans from behind gilded screens.
His mother gave birth to beautiful twins. He was ashamed.

&#42;  &#42;  &#42;

The prince came of age and ascended the throne. Decreed that the queen mother be banished forever, her twins be put to death, and a certain eunuch be cut into a thousand pieces. "Never again shall I see that woman," he swore, "unless it be under Nine Springs, where the dead convene."

He ruled over a vast kingdom. A haggard woman haunted his dreams.

The royal guards sought and found Nine Springs, dug a tunnel beneath it. The king descended underground, beheld a snow-haired woman.
He fell on his knees at her feet. She bathed his face with tears.

# The Lovers of Teruel

She thought him dead
As bells tolled
her wedding to another man
he materialized
and requested a kiss
She refused
He collapsed at her feet

*They once flew down*
*gargoyled corridors*
*Laughter chimed echoing*
*off Mudejar towers*

On her wedding night
from the bejeweled bed
her husband chided her
for not having kissed
the man who died for her
*She sank to the floor*
*in her white veil*

The next day
at his funeral
she lifted her bridal veil
kissed him
died holding him
*A thunderstorm brewed*
*in half barren mountains*
*The river carried away*
*trampled rose petals*

The lovers rest on
sarcophagus lids
marble hands eternally
reaching for each other

Shakespeare knew
no one could die of love
without poison or an ornate dagger
He moved them to Verona
Married them as blissful teens
Immortalized regret

# Frida With Hummingbirds

A diary entry recounts her steamy encounter with Doroti in a Paris hotel. Sometimes she went after women her husband had bedded. The Mayans beheaded winners of the ballgame. Hummingbirds sing by diving. The air sculpted into songs, piped by ruby and emerald tail feathers.

Her husband dissected the hummingbirds to extract aphrodisiacs.

Pyramids glowed in the jungle. Beasts of prey held human hearts in cavernous mouths. Next to the amputation done to her right leg, illustrated in a French medical book, she scribbled her pain. The hummingbirds watched her. She shivered, wrote to a friend to ask for coconut candies.

A lacquer box contains eleven stuffed hummingbirds, beneath her letter of lamentation.

## Casanova: A Translation from Fellini

Famous for private entertainment and winning public competitions of copulation, he received an invitation from an anonymous dignitary. He rode for miles in the gondola to perform. After saluting, he swirled, the curious nun on his waist, his scarlet cape a flag pulling eyes behind carved peeping holes. When the show ended, he asked for permission to present his essays and inventions. His voice echoed in the deserted monastery.

✻        ✻        ✻

Her Royal Highness in disguise put a slender finger on his lips. She played the cello in a string quartet, in the marble court lit by crystal chandeliers. The deep calm of the cello overcame him. He fled into the rose garden, tears streaming. He planned a future with her. She departed in a gilded carriage while he slept.

✻        ✻        ✻

Old and gray, he begged for food. The same waltz haunted his dreams each night. A procession of red hooded priests. Then the princess stepped out of a golden carriage. Breaking into the shop where she was displayed, he once made love to her in despair. She jerked her painted head, reached out a porcelain hand. He held it. They danced.

## The Mirror's Edge

She slept with the bear to relieve herself of the burden of purity
to travel the world alone with only a backpack.

Apple trees lit up with ten thousand sun-filled blossoms.

She winced when he pinched her and praised her legs. He suggested
that she see a doctor for her unnatural fear of the inevitable.

White petals blew in the wind as church bells tolled.

He undressed her and pushed her down. It hurt but she did not
make a sound. He was disappointed by the absence of blood.

White petals were trampled into mud.

Bears do not turn into handsome princes. He turned into a half bald man
with a leather bound journal, in which he noted her various imperfections.

# A Night in Athens

She sipped ouzo and turned away
Each time to avoid his kiss
Dark curls towered over her
Bronze arms twirled her

\*        \*        \*

The hall surged with lithe limbs
The air pulsed with loud beats
Mirrors echoed peach blossom smiles
Couples laughing danced into the pool

\*        \*        \*

He parked on a deserted beach
Forced himself on her as Orion blazed
Her jeans' zipper scratched his penis
He yelped and agreed to stop

\*        \*        \*

Icelandic girls burst into the hostel room
One blonde offered her bottled water
The other took out a camera
Insisted on taking her photograph

## San Francisco Bay at Night

A white tern dives
into dark satin embroidered
by lights
Bare masts     empty ships
on quivering ripples

Rhythmic tides drown a beach of footprints

Sand on sand reposes
leading to the desert
of lights
of hearts counting gold coins
in frosted dreams

Rhythmic tides drown a beach of footprints

Under a sky of sparkling
go-pieces     kiss me
Stranger
before I open my eyes
and dive into the dark

light-embroidered satin

## Neighbors in Bathrobes

Geese honk across inky sky. Flames hiss in the fireplace. The corridor re-sounds with thuds. She puts on a purple silk robe. A plump brown cat launches itself at the stocky man's door across the hall, scratches it with one paw. An old woman in white pantsuit brings a bowl of milk. The cat drinks, resumes thumps.

She sits in a field of irises, observes a mountain translucent on the hori-zon. A tall man with flowing hair kneels to kiss her toes.

\*  \*  \*

Loud banging on the door across the hall.
Someone chuckles over a walky-talky.
Several doors open and close.
Flashing of bathrobes: red, green, white, blue.

\*  \*  \*

The sky folds into blowing gauze curtains. The old woman frowns at her on the wooden stairs. In the laundry room, the stocky man in a bright yellow bathrobe. He fusses over seven glass vials, bubbling in seven shades of blue, avoids her gaze. She asks if his cat is pregnant. *No,* he snaps, *both girls are fine.*

Two brown cats press their faces against the sliding glass door to his balcony, strewn with reflections of naked apple branches.

# Nocturne II

A star beckons
from the mountain
in a dark forest

I climb mud slopes
claw up shear cliffs

A silver portal opens
to the hidden garden
of unearthly green orchids

I plunge into the icy lake
Brown milfoil chokes me

I float on the pale moon

# Frondescence

Owls hoot in code as stars blink
She tells a man she no longer loves him
He snores on without pause

Scarlet flycatchers splatter droppings
The fig tree shudders in sallow leaves
Green fists conceal inner changes

She pulls up her long hair from the ground
Reunites with the stranger from a train
Cherry blossom petals rain down

Plastic people flaunt their perfect faces
A hummingbird taunts her
The quiver of uneven eyelids

She whispers in the stranger's arms
*I have not told you everything*
Cobweb wraps her in a cocoon

He melts into indigo light
The figs have vanished
Stolen in the dead of night

*The Universe has many secrets*
She dives down a green cliff
Into a labyrinth of light

# Winter Seascape

Cacti-covered hills drop down
toward jade-skirted sapphire sea

Oil rigs roost on hazy horizon
White mansions dream on cliff ledges

Scattered domes of blue oaks
fasten cracked earth

\*          \*          \*

Winter sun in late afternoon
casts a blinding tunnel in the sea
It follows me along the shore

Translucent waves rush the beach
to polish veined dark pebbles

\*          \*          \*

We have sailed past each other in the dark

The moon's silver candle lights the ocean
Water pulses loud with invitation

I feel the tug of star tides
anchoring me in an invisible harbor

## Minuet

In summer's frondescence
I walk on the lake of your dream
I reach out my hands
We begin a swirling dance

We are light as the air
Our shadows fall on a jade mirror
Underwater grass follows our tempo
sends sparks of chords

Suddenly we are flying
invisible as spirits
The forest becomes a tiny dot
Our song has no echoes

# Ever After

*The Universe is an invisible dark web*
*knotted into sparkling galaxies*

The princess wept alone in a hut
Her long dark hair scented by green orchids
Her chariot pulled by tigers and leopards

*The Universe grew from nothingness*
*It may decay into nothingness*

The prince sailed seven seas incognito
Seeking new challenges and merry damsels
They played card games in night trains

*The Universe may end in a Big Crunch*
*The birth of a new Universe*

Indian hawthorn blossoms burst pink
through dense hedges of winter green
Waves crash white into black caves

*The Universe is not a flower*
*We are dewdrops on a petal*

The Milky Way rises over an unlit hut
A gravity-bound marble among the countless
Each contains a hundred billion stars

# Flowers in the Mirror

She bolts the door to meet the man inside the mirror. Peach blossom petals rain down. Long hair drapes down his bare shoulders. He beckons, a knowing smile on his face luminous as jade. A siren shrieks by outside.

*Fledglings abandoned the nest as leaves yellowed on the phoenix tree.*

Love is an illusion, born of misunderstandings. She dreams in the empty house. Aliens land in LA, and uproot palm trees to use as toothpicks. She is a tiny fish on a silver platter, screaming, voiceless.

*White-ridged mountains: sprigs of snowflakes from the space station.*

Sunlight throbs translucent hollows of morning glories. Someone hugs her from behind. She is afraid to open her eyes. The mind blooms. The moon ripples in the water, a corridor from here to eternity.

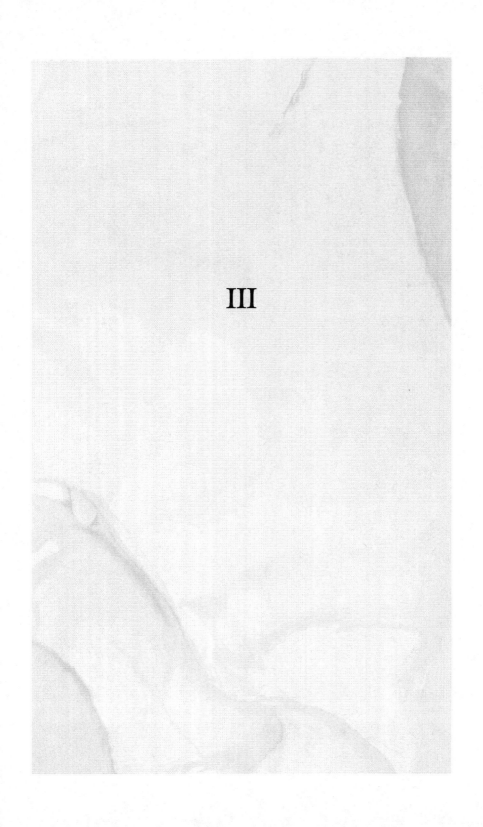

III

# Hidden

Yuccas bloom moonbeam torches
Mark the mountain path at noon

Travel without a name

Black mustard spreads golden foreboding
Midnight sage spouts tiny indigo sails

Breathe in scents as wild bees dance

Primrose's pink crosses light up the slope
facing a valley of white alders

The stream gurgles unseen
Suddenly on the overgrown ledge
a brown bear cub

## The Visitation

The doctor said it was nerve disorder
that caused noises in the ears
Schumann listened and went mad

The voices chose him because of his music
A thousand fairies dancing in shoes of flame

It created a riot in their world
They wanted him to stop

They came through the piano's
black and white doors
They stitched his mind into a maze

## Shadow Test

Newton stuck a needle in one of his eyes
to change the retina's shape
You wonder what you have done

Darkness seeps into your eyes
The sun seems bright as ever
You want to howl and start a fire

Once you saw people's faces narrow
into crescents in a departing train
You were seven years old

had lost your ticket and cried
Something has returned
It is transmuting everything

Leaves and slits between your fingers
Everywhere the crescent shadows
You cover each eye in turn

Shadows sharpen into thread-thin hooks
You shudder and realize
you are being examined by the moon

# Children's Game in Baghdad

A small boy jumped off corpses for fun. He explained to his mother that they were nothing. Dogs ate them. She told him that every dead man had a mother waiting for him to come home. He fell asleep in her arms.

The sun bled into charred gum trees.

She brought him to work. Photographed the green zone for a newspaper. A bomb sprayed them with shrapnel. She couldn't stop shaking. He said it's OK, not his first bomb. His school was shelled the week before.

Once upon a time rose petals rained down.

She couldn't stop thinking of his lack of feelings. He whispered that all his friends jumped off dead bodies. In her dream, her husband handed her the Sumerian tablet he died protecting. The cuneiforms shifted into a pair of wings.

# Green Stars

Hathor planted the endless sky
with turquoise and malachite
The Nile fertilizes myriad cycles
feeding successive conquerors

The desert whispers an eroding song
around mighty pyramids
Fire and smoke ravish
ruins of Cleopatra's dreams

On the gates to tomb chambers
Hathor pauses in frescoed serenity
In the souk a boy on a dark horse
glares at fawning tourists

Beyond bells of mosques
the desert sings an eroding song
under green stars of Egypt

## An Ancient Ice Bridge Breaks


Polar bears whimper in melting dreams. Eskimo villages fall into the sea.
Earth's whispering green hair is thinned to make disposable chopsticks.

Trucks crisscross the country. Hundred year storms strike every year.
Fire ants invade pumpkin patches. Mercury laces rivers.

Earth's white wings shimmer and shrink. Clouds meld acid into the ocean.
The autistic girl screams, draws dolphins weeping blood into dark waves.

# Contact

Dolphin males die young
Mercury rains into the ocean
Females pass the poison to babies
through breast milk

Taiji fishermen drive dolphins
into a secret cove
harpoon two thousand
for school lunches

A gray whale sings
rises from turquoise waves
eyes a Baja fisherman
lifts his boat
glistening into the air
puts it down
gently

# The Beetle from Outer Space

A tiny rock wandered off Kuiper Belt, descended to Earth in a fireball. It splashed into Great Sand Sea, made a molten lake of bubbling sand. The sand cooled, became yellow green glass. It was carved into a scarab beetle, worn on a necklace by young Tutankhamun for three thousand years.

A water boy found steps leading to Tutankhamun's tomb. Howard Carter made a tiny breach in the doorway, peered in by a candle's light.

*May your spirit live*
*May you spend millions of years*
*You who love Thebes*
*Sitting with your face to the north wind*
*Your eyes beholding happiness*

A faint cry, almost human. A cobra in the birdcage, Carter's canary in its mouth.

Lord Carnarvon hired Carter, was bitten by a mosquito, slashed the bite while shaving, died of blood poisoning. Carter saw jackals in the likeness of Anubis for the first time in the desert.

Carter's friend Ingham was gifted a mummified hand as paperweight. On its wrist, a scarab bracelet inscribed with hieroglyphs. Ingham's house burned down, was rebuilt. A flood followed. As foretold by the inscription.

*My mother Sky*
*spread yourself over me*
*so that I may be placed*
*among the imperishable stars*

# Walking on Mars

The red planet veils with sunset
filtered blue by its tiny dust grains

*Two dolphins arch above waves*
*Their wet bodies mirror the sun*

Walking on silent Mars I ache
for the blue planet's red sunset

*A flute's languid call in moist air*
*Indigo rain of jacaranda flowers*

## Saturn's Moons

Cronus ate his own children
Planets became echoes to the Sun
in the cold hall
without walls

Geysers erupt on snowy Enceladus
Hydrocarbon stirs in Titan's lakes
Cronus fell through
history's mirror

became Saturn to sow seeds
Life brews on Titan and Enceladus
Stone bursts into flowers
in gravity's garden

# Seascape at Santa Monica

Green waves roar into white oblivion
laughing their heads off in drooping light

Sunset ignites tiny sails
on washed-up sargasso loops

Evening tide heaves metallic sheen
erases rose tendrils on a glossy mirror

Smog conceals the Milky Way
The Ferris wheel bleeds neon

The moon forges a shimmering corridor
in a dark sea of thunderous doors

## Thousands of Years at a Glance

African lilies trumpet indigo
hymn inaudible to human ears

*Seeds were planted for the first time*
*one hundred seventeen centuries ago*

Ideograms once carved on turtle shells
stare back from a billion screens

*A thousand-year-old cherry tree*
*bursts into a waterfall of blossoms*

Jacarandas suit up in green fern feathers
The crescent ferries cloud-oared dreams

*Rockets began as fireworks in China*
*Two millennia rushed by in smoke*

Lotuses emblazon the goddess headdress
on the skull of the Scythian warrior queen

*An iron hook in an eagle's shape*
*buried with thirty iron arrowheads*

She swept the Silk Road on a roan stallion
Her azure cape gathering starlight

*Thirty-six other civilizations might exist*
*in the Milky Way's vast wheel of stars*

It would be a nightmare
if all our wishes came true

# Migration

Water falls in a thousand folds of crystal silk
You see shadows robed in white
follow them and they turn
in a labyrinth of winged branches

Untangle your hair from the willow
Your boat sails down a smooth dark river
lit by a torch of sandalwood fire
A man wreathed in scarlet feathers
towers over the bow

Lie down and hear water
glide beneath you
Banana leaves brush your face
Nudes painted with rainbow waves
bend down from vine-tasseled bridges
Their faces flooded by the moon

The boat stops as drums rumble
through the singing wind
You fall on your knees
A monarch butterfly lands
on your forehead

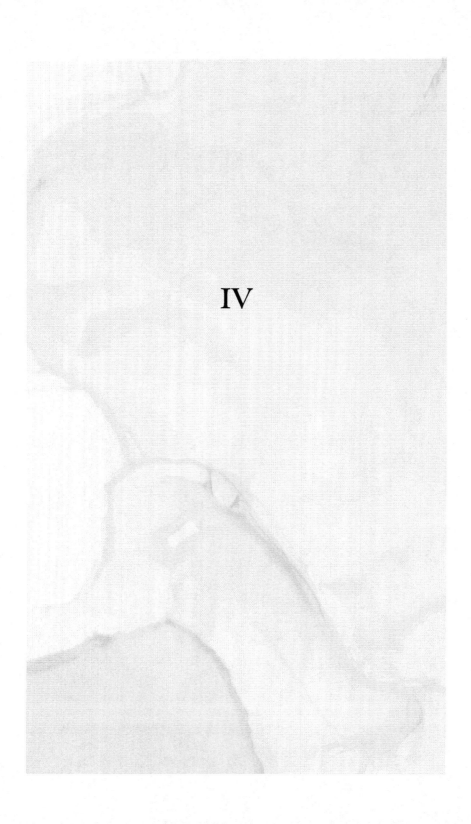

IV

# Horse by the Mountain Stream

Wild orchids bloom purple and white
against a blue stream
Their scent opens the window
into a world without consequences

A headmistress chastises the cook
for complaining about improper oil
on the other side of Earth
Children die from eating the school lunch
cooked with oil from an insecticide jug

The stream rushes down from snow
atop rocky mountains where cows
sway gently in the wind
making a symphony with their bells
They live in meadow paradise
until led to the slaughter house

Joshua Bell plays the Chaconne
in a subway station
No one stops long enough to listen

Bach wrote the Chaconne
to cleanse souls for the journey
to forgotten dreams

A path digs through tall grass
by the stream dashing toward a valley
where Mahler composed
Das Lied von der Erde

When someone goes away to the mountains
never to return
what do they find

by the chill mountain stream
The black horse drank
was sent back galloping
For a second I fear it will charge me
It stops in front of me
I pat its dark mane
It begins to eat sunlit grass

# August Dream

Why was my father wearing a blue formal jacket
when it was so hot? It was summer in Oklahoma
and over a hundred degrees. He wanted to know

where he was. I explained that he could not return
to this world since his body no longer existed.

He seemed relieved. I saw him being cremated
three years before as they played "The Rebirth
of the Phoenix" on rustic trumpets.

I buried his ashes in a white jade box on a mountain.

# Immortality

My father washed his only shirt at night
dried it by the fire in a haunted house
by a white river in the mountains
He pours osmanthus black tea
into blue porcelain cups in my dreams
five years after his death

My mother gazed at Venus at dawn
as she cleaned chamber pots
for wealthy classmates
She bought me a diamond ring
a few months before she died
She had wanted one all her life

I watch peonies of white clouds
bloom in the Maya blue sky
contemplate the filaments of galaxies
and the voids they frame
The Universe expands
My son promises to build me a spaceship

## Sam's Plan

The little planet is green
With lemonade ocean
Boys are blue
Girls are pink
They are ant-size

Forests are purple
Sky is indigo

If a spaceship approaches
It will shrink to mushroom size
Astronauts will be tiny
Boys blue
Girls pink

Little machines will help little people
Each is good and where it belongs
One will harvest lightning for electricity
Another will make sandwiches

I will invent the machines
When I land on that planet

## Sam's Questions

Why does a monkey toss acorns
onto the stone riverbank
Where did thrushes learn to sing
How did music begin

Why does Ma mean Mother
in every human language
Why was a princess called Tiger Lily
How are words made

Where did the world come from
How did leaves begin to eat sunlight
What would I see
from the dark side of the Moon

## Supermoon

Pearl eye of the cloud dragon
kindles pink lanterns on the orchid tree

My son's arms around me
In a beam of liquid light

We are immortals to mayflies
Let this be enough

# Seascape at South Padre Island

Dolphins part sargasso curtains
to observe
ice mountains in the sky
shape-shifting into a brush-painted
pine forest

Salt-sprayed men extend themselves
into the sea
through fishing poles
Buckets fill with striped fish
gasping to death

Scarlet sunset

A procession along the jetty
Black-suited men and women
each holding a long stem red rose
Followed by a young blonde
A white-gowned infant in her arms

Our blood speaks the tongue
of the gleaming sea
Dolphins the leaping angels
of the continuum
etch it on scrolls of moonlit water

## Gifted with Beauty

My daughter flailed her arms
I swam to her
She jumped on me

dragged me under water
I sank in shock
brushed the cold hand of death

pushed her off and shouted for help
Nearby youths laughed
I yelled that it was no joke

They pulled me up
We found my daughter
beaming on the shore

at the waterfall splashing
into emerald depths
A rainbow

My autistic daughter
lighted up the dark pond
with her smile

Later they found a pink water shoe
at the bottom of the pond
She had wanted me to fetch it

# Snow Angel

Perhaps there is nothing
beyond what we see
A forest in mist
A forest in snow
Someone climbs out of a stranded car
wearing a scarlet hat

The details astound
A translucent white gown
Small bare feet
A smile on the soft face

You rub your eyes
You are sitting on the sofa
watching a Christmas commercial
You are standing outside
in the snowstorm with a girl's name

Your car slipped off the road
heading for a tree but stopped
one inch before it
Something flew out of white branches

You climbed out of the car
You looked up and saw a flash
Perhaps there is nothing
beyond that
You feel snow on your bare feet
You wonder whose dream this is
Each night the sky is tiled anew
by seamless dreams

# Transformation

My father as a child
sat alone in a dark room
by his father's deathbed
The oil lamp's flame quivered
There was no wind
His father stopped breathing

Seventy-five years later
my father slept
as the sun rose
When he left his body
I was ten thousand miles away
across the ocean
The sun shone on us both

The concrete sidewalk
was a sun-jeweled landscape

## The Burren

The cream pony gallops towards me
on the way to the hilltop cemetery

A thousand years of gravestones surround
black bones of a forgotten church

Dogs bark and someone rustles in the grass
Beyond the sunlit landscape the sea grays

    *       *       *

Waves crash into cliffs and bloom
hundreds of feet into the air

Unnamed wildflowers whisper my name
My heart freezes on the deserted trail

Vertical cliffs wall up the sea
A vast bowl stretches into the horizon

No ship on the horizon no one waits for me
I saw it all in the pony's green eyes

    *       *       *

The village hugs a river cascade
dropping hundreds of bolts of silk

Along the forest canopy's crack
a little stream reflects fuchsia foxgloves

A tree daisy watches with ten thousand eyes
My swan dream turns into a butterfly

Heed not the call from the sea
Cliff-hung wildflowers cup moonlight

# Fuerteventura at Night

Waves link and knot undulating light
The ocean thunders in sunset's fire
The Milky Way rises from dark ashes

Conquerors landed on a coral beach
followed the river to villages
sold the natives as slaves to pirates

Sagittarius slays Scorpius each night
A massive black hole lurks behind him
The Milky Way's throbbing heart

The ring of desert-mountains hid
an ancient cradle of vision dreamers

The Milky Way arches across the sky
falls between two mountains
Obsidian guards to the celestial portal

Andromeda hesitates
between Cassiopeia and Pegasus
An entire galaxy blazing on her right wrist

# The Butterfly

The day after I buried my father's ashes on a mountain, a giant black swallowtail languidly glided over camellias. My father was old Wang. The first Wang, a dashing teenage prince, died in 547 BC. Thirty years later, the ailing king dreamed the prince descended on a white crane, playing the sheng.

I dreamed of the future, where a man stands trial for loneliness. I defend him, noting that, in my own time, so long ago, loneliness was the human condition. In another dream, I consort with an intimate stranger. He holds my hands, gazes into my eyes, in a valley of towering statues ringed by turquoise mountains.

Legend made the prince immortal. He ascended in moon-glow from a mountain-top, his white robe dancing the wind. The butterfly was Zhuang Zi dreaming this world. Or my father, returning with dark wings embossed with silver and emerald.

Moonlight fills me through shut eyelids. I melt into the lucid stream.

# Epiphany

Rocks bounce backlit water-drops
sparkling gnats of time
Ferns line up luminous banners

The temple of ancient pine grove
hushes thoughts

My son closes his eyes to listen
to the waterfall's song
brightens it with his presence

# Forecasts

Humans may evolve into machines. The internet weaves insidious threads. Roses bloom by empty benches. Poetry fades on dusty shelves. Aliens may land in Kansas tomorrow, or discover the jazz from Voyager a thousand years from now.

Computers can impersonate the dead. Machines may become sentient, keep humans in zoos, or erase all biological organisms. In another universe, an ash tree's roots span a continent and shimmer into the air, weaving paths to other planets.

The elite may invent immortality, herd the masses into concentration camps. Aliens may arrive with silver arks to ferry refugees to Andromeda. The Earth is an egg about to hatch. We are the gametes.

The Universe will shrink back into a tiny bubble, or dissipate into space-time foam. Only the soul can escape through a wormhole.

# Notes

"Black Roses": The first part refers to a cosmology conference in the 1980s, during which the discovery of the periodicity in the distribution of galaxies in the Universe was presented on slides and in the form of electronic music. The last part refers to "The Happy Prince" written by Oscar Wilde. There is no evidence that Hans Christian Andersen hated children.

"Bach's Chaconne" was inspired by the final movement of *Partita for Violin No. 2 in D Minor* written by Johann Sebastian Bach, Ciaccona (usually referred to as "Chaconne" as in French).

"The Nun and the Prince" was inspired by characters from *Dream of the Red Mansion*, the Chinese novel classic by Cao Xueqin from the 18th century.

"Nine Springs" was inspired by an episode from ancient Chinese history.

"Casanova: A Translation from Fellini" is based on the 1976 Italian film by director Federico Fellini, *Fellini's Casanova* (*Il Casanova di Federico Fellini*), an adaptation of the autobiography of Giacomo Casanova from the 18th century.

"Children's Game in Baghdad" is mostly based on a news story reported by the National Public Radio.

"The Beetle from Outer Space": The first italicized stanza is from the inscription on the Wishing Cup of Tutankhamun, and the second is the prayer to the Sky Goddess Nut found on the lids of New Kingdom coffins.

"Saturn's Moons" was inspired by the Cassini Probe launched by NASA in 1997. It orbited Saturn from 2004 until 2017, when it was deliberately destroyed in Saturn's atmosphere. This was done to avoid Cassini's eventual orbit decay and its subsequent possible collision with Saturn's moons Enceladus or Titan. Such a collision would contaminate the possibly life-supporting environments on these moons (key findings of Cassini).

"The Butterly": The crown prince Ji Jin during the Zhou Dynasty became known as Wang Zi-Qiao (~567 BC - 547 BC) in history. Being extremely gifted, learned, and wise, he was punished for frank assessments and inconvenient advice to the king, and became a commoner, and the original ancestor of people with the family name "Wang" (meaning "royal"). He was fond of playing the sheng (a mouth-blown free reed instrument consisting of vertical pipes), and said to have ascended to Heaven riding a white crane. In Taoism, the stature of Zhuang Zi (~369 BC - ~286 BC) is second only to its founder, Lao Zi (604 BC - 531 BC). When Zhuang Zi woke up from a dream in which he was a butterfly, he wondered if he was actually the butterfly dreaming of being a man.

## The Author

Yun Wang is the author of poetry books *The Book of Totality* (Salmon Poetry Press, 2015) and *The Book of Jade* (Winner of the 15th Nicholas Roerich Poetry Prize, Story Line Press, 2002), and the book of poetry translations *Dreaming of Fallen Blossoms: Tune Poems of Su Dong-Po* (White Pine Press, 2019). Wang's poems have been published in numerous literary journals, including *The Kenyon Review, Prairie Schooner, Cimarron Review, Salamander Magazine, Valparaiso Poetry Review, Green Mountains Review,* and *International Quarterly.* Her translations of classical Chinese poetry have been published in *The Kenyon Review Online, Salamander Magazine, Poetry Canada Review, Willow Springs, Kyoto Journal, Bat City Review, Xavier Review, Connotation Press,* and elsewhere. Wang was born in China, and came to the U.S. for graduate school in 1985. She is an astrophysicist at California Institute of Technology, currently focusing on developing space missions to explore the Universe.

# THE WHITE PINE PRESS POETRY PRIZE

Vol. 26: *The Book of Mirrors* by Yun Wang. Selected by Jennifer Kwon Dobbs.

Vol. 25: *Aflame* by Gary McDowell. Selected by Sean Thomas Dougherty.

Vol. 24: *Our Age of Anxiety* by Henry Israeli. Selected by Kathleen McGookey.

Vol. 23: *Secure Your Own Mask* by Shaindel Beers. Selected by Alan Michael Parker.

Vol. 22: *Bread From a Stranger's Oven* by Janlori Goldman. Selected by Laure-Anne Bosselaar.

Vol. 21: *The Brighter House* by Kim Garcia. Selected by Jericho Brown.

Vol. 20: *Some Girls* by Janet McNally. Selected by Ellen Bass.

Vol. 19: *Risk* by Tim Skeen. Selected by Gary Young.

Vol. 18: *What Euclid's Third Axiom Neglects to Mention About Circles* by Carolyn Moore. Selected by Patricia Spears Jones.

Vol. 17: *Notes from the Journey Westward* by Joe Wilkins. Selected by Samuel Green.

Vol. 16: *Still Life* by Alexander Long. Selected by Aliki Barnstone.

Vol. 15: *Letters From the Emily Dickinson Room* by Kelli Russell Agodon. Selected by Carl Dennis.

Vol. 14: *In Advance of All Parting* by Ansie Baird. Selected by Roo Borson.

Vol. 13: *Ghost Alphabet* by Al Maginnes. Selected by Peter Johnson.

Vol. 12: *Paper Pavilion* by Jennifer Kwon Dobbs. Selected by Genie Zeiger.

Vol. 11: *The Trouble with a Short Horse in Montana* by Roy Bentley. Selected by John Brandi.

Vol. 10: *The Precarious Rhetoric of Angels* by George Looney. Selected by Nin Andrews.

Vol. 9: *The Burning Point* by Frances Richey. Selected by Stephen Corey.

Vol. 8: *Watching Cartoons Before Attending A Funeral* by John Surowiecki. Selected by C.D. Wright.

Vol. 7: *My Father Sings, To My Embarrassment* by Sandra Castillo. Selected by Cornelius Eady.

Vol. 6: *If Not For These Wrinkles of Darkness* by Stephen Frech. Selected by Pattiann Rogers.

Vol. 5: *Trouble in History* by David Keller. Selected by Pablo Medina.

Vol. 4: *Winged Insects* by Joel Long. Selected by Jane Hirshfield.

Vol. 3: *A Gathering of Mother Tongues* by Jacqueline Joan Johnson. Selected by Maurice Kenny.

Vol. 2: *Bodily Course* by Deborah Gorlin. Selected by Mekeel McBride.

Vol. 1: *Zoo & Cathedral* by Nancy Johnson. Selected by David St. John.